God, Love & Divorce

A Journey of Self-Discovery

Danita M. Sanders

ISBN-10: 0692549331
ISBN-13: 978-0692549339

DEDICATION

Dedicated to Kyrie, Kiera, Kaelin, and Kiersten; the reasons why I am driven and want to be the best I can be. You inspire me and love you beyond any words can say!

CONTENTS

ACKNOWLEDGMENTS

There are just so many people to thank for their support in this process. Charge it to my head and not my heart if I do not name you specifically but there are some key individuals I must acknowledge and in no particular order.

To Shannon Y. Tanner, you were my birthing coach for this dream. You were key to my recovery with your book, *Worthy*. Your generosity put this vision into reality!

To Kristin Hargraves, Brook Chalfant, Melissa Richardson, Shanna Brown, Kim Woods, and Heather Laing, thank you for your support, encouragement, accountability, and most of all, your friendship.

To "Team Pray with Us", Adiya Johnson, Leesha Archie, and Ninalynn Bradshaw, thank you for your prayers. You are indeed prayer warriors.

Thank you to Wave Church and Pastors Steve & Sharon Kelly. This was the place God would use to build me back up.

Thank you to the father of my beautiful children. Thank you for becoming my friend even after our marriage ended.

"I count him braver who overcomes his desires than him who conquers his enemies, for the hardest victory is over self."
— Aristotle

Introduction
Welcome to the Journey

Have you ever been looking for something around the house? I mean diligently searching and it just doesn't seem to be anywhere. Ever been there? Then a few days or weeks go by and in the process of looking for something else, you find that thing you were originally looking for staring you right in your face. It was there all along. This has happened to me so many times I have lost count.

In 2009, this happened to me when I was looking for something rather important or should I say someone important. I was looking for myself. Caught up in the role of wife and stay-at-home mom, there were moments of feeling something drawing me beyond those titles. When my husband was at work and my kids were out playing, I was left to face Danita, and it became a really intentional time. It went from who is this woman born Danita Myanne Holmes to how did I become this now wife and mother, Danita Myanne Sanders? God was determined to continue something in me that He started a long time ago. But life and all its moments and experiences kept me distracted from me. There were times that I admittedly chose to deal with anything but what was going on inside of me. There was a draw, a pull to something more, something deeper. Who was I? Why was I here?

We can find ourselves haphazardly going through life and begin to feel the chaos, the frustration. It feels like everything and everyone around us is frustrating us, but we are really frustrated with ourselves. We are either trying too hard to please others or being someone we are not. It is the classic signs of SMIA: self-missing in action. Through the changing of life's seasons and life's experiences, we have buried ourselves beneath a pile of duties, titles, and so many of other things. When you don't know who you are, you can take on personalities and character traits that are not you. Somehow, some way, we know something within ourselves is crying out. We are changing, evolving, transforming. We are doing life as a single person, spouse, parent, employee, and/or business owner and finding ourselves irritated or frustrated at times and not knowing why.

Well I was looking for me, hard. I was doing everything I

knew to do and was still finding myself frustrated and oftentimes lost. But in the middle of searching for me, I happened upon something else. I happened upon love. I was doing life and including God, but there came a shift. I realized I needed to do life with God and through God, not just including Him here and there. I knew that God loved me, but what did that look like? My family has always been, well, my family. There was no denying their love for me or our love for each other. But there was something missing for me. I needed something more meaningful, something deeper.

One Saturday morning, I spent time with some of the girls from church. At first, the weather did not look like this beach experience was going to happen, but then things cleared up, and I ventured out. Sitting at the beach, just enjoying the sun and the breeze, not to mention some great company, I realized life was great, full, whole. It had been a year since the divorce. Not a long time to some, but for me, it was a productive year. It was the year that I found her. It was the year I found me.

Hanging with the girls at the beach that day had just been icing on the "discovery of me" cake. This has been a rather long journey with a lot of stops and starts, a lot of roadblocks and caution signs, and a few accidents. But something happened within me after the divorce. Anything in the way of this journey had to go, and it did. However it was to happen, transformation and rediscovery were here, and there was no stopping it. I saw my ex-husband move on with his life, and I saw a terribly toxic relationship ending before it ever truly ended. I found myself asking why I was not moving forward. The marriage had been over for more than three years and the divorce was final.

It took a long time to find safe ground with new friends, old friends, and most importantly me. When you have been deeply wounded beyond words, it is difficult to feel safe with anyone. Life still felt like it was in neutral. Sometimes there was what seemed like forward progress only to be halted again.

Then things began to take a huge turn. I followed Bishop T. D. Jakes and his transformation series at the beginning of 2014 and while asking myself the questions on moving forward with my life, I felt like God was saying it was time. So parts and pieces began to move and shift in my life. Roadblocks were being bulldozed out of my way, and God began closing doors that I did not have the strength to close.

Before I knew it, in what seemed like months, I was loving life. Everything was new and fresh. I could smile, and it came from the inside of who I was and not from what was happening around me. Everything did not have to be going well for me to find a reason to smile.

More often than not, I am optimistic and hopeful about every day I open my eyes. I can think of at least five things that were not perfect or issues that needed to be addressed, yet I still had the greatest sense of peace and joy from well within myself. I knew that things were going to be okay.

So what was the change? What was difference? It was that I had finally silenced every voice in my life except God. The difference was I had finally found clarity and could see where I was battling between the person everybody else around me said I was and the person I truly was at my core. God was peeling away the layers and silencing the voices. I was waking up to the dawn of the real me, the me who was always there.

I will never forget God giving me a vision of me holding on to His hand. As He was lifting me into the air, the beautiful layered dress I had been wearing fell away into the same dress, same style but different color. The more He would lift me, the more the dress changed colors as each layer fell away. I had forgotten that vision until this year. I was reminded of it again, and this time, the vision was the same, but I could hear God naming names and labels as the dress would fall away and change colors: broken, unlovable, worthless, inadequate, not good enough, over thinker, super spiritual, etc. The higher I went, the more labels He named. When He said the final name of the last thing that represented the last dress, the last layer I would shed, my dress was white. It was the first time I had seen white in the vision. Then He began to give me new names: loved, adored, beautiful, creative, talented, worthy, whole, complete, Danita, Mine! God was showing me that the higher I went in my relationship with Him, the more He would peel away the labels and residue of the people and their personalities that had tainted who I was.

Some labels I could not dismiss: daughter, caregiver, mother, wife, entrepreneur, etc., but the more labels and titles I took on, the more I lost me at the core. I spent a great deal of time during my marriage building and strengthening my relationship with God. Being a full-time mom, I was able to read, study, and find things out about God for myself. There were always challenges, as there should be, but the battle between who I was and who I was growing to be grew stronger. When the separation and eventually the divorce took place, I thought I was lost forever. I did not think I could ever recover. Not anymore. I now know that recovery is possible, and you can come out on the other side of any challenge, tragedy, or obstacle better, stronger, wiser, and more determined if you choose to do the work and do it well.

My divorce was the most painful thing I had ever endured. But it gave me the most beautiful and precious gift. It gave me, me. When you don't even have control over you, the one thing you should have some degree of control over, turmoil can run and cause all kinds of identity confusion. There was nothing I wanted more than to be a great wife and a great mother. Failure was not an option for me, and it was not an option for my ex-husband. I believe we both gave it our best effort, but he would be the first to tell you that we just could not get on the same page.

So let me be clear. This book is not about fault finding or placing blame. We both had our parts to play. So if you are looking for dirty laundry to be aired, you bought the wrong book. This book is about choosing love because love is choosing you. God's love is always choosing you. It is about choosing to live when spiritual death and emotional death are imminent. It's about things falling apart just to fall back into a better place. It's about finding you and loving you the way God loves you because it is then and only then that we can truly love others.

This book is for anyone who has been through divorce, facing divorce, having marriage issues/problems, and friends and/or family of someone who fit in the previous categories. I am hoping to enlighten some and give hope to many. I am hoping to inspire some to fight for their families and others to support their friends and families as they fight. But if divorce has happened or is inevitable, divorce is not the end of the story. It is a chapter in the book: a chapter on life, love, death, and restoration.

This book is also for anyone who knows what it feels like to be looking for deeper than they've ever seen. Maybe you've felt lost just walking through life. Instead of thriving, you've just been surviving. So much of what we try to fill ourselves with to replace the indescribable void can never give us what we are looking for in this life.

What we are searching diligently for can only be found within. God, our loving creator, placed all that we need within us and when we discover Him and then embrace His love, He then shows us who we are. That is what I found while walking through my divorce, I found me. God loved me before I got married. He loved me during my marriage, and He loved me even more afterwards. It was the love that gave me the strength to not only own up to areas where I fell short in life, but also give me the compassion for myself to say life was not over. It was just beginning again.

Let's take a walk through the art of self-discovery. It won't look the same for us all. Our paths may be different, but the end result is the same. The end result is a stronger, loving, more compassionate version of who you are truly meant to be.

<u>Reflection</u>

Do you feel there is something within you crying out? Do you feel lost or find yourself questioning your identity? Do you feel like there is something more you should be doing or feel called to do more than you are currently doing? God may be trying to get your attention and woo you back to Him so He can teach you who you are and what your purpose is.

<u>Notes</u>

Here is where you can jot down answers to the Reflection questions and any additional thoughts.

THE ART OF DISCOVERY

Transformation is a process, and as life happens there are tons of ups and downs. It's a journey of discovery - there are moments on mountaintops and moments in deep valleys of despair.

Rick Warren

"The voyage of discovery is not in seeking new landscapes but in having new eyes."

-Marcel Proust

1 LOOK WHO I FOUND

I love a good movie. Action and adventure are usually my favorites, not to mention most Disney movies, but every once in a while, I can get into a chick flick. Runaway Bride, starring Julia Roberts as Maggie Carpenter and Richard Gere as Ike Graham, is one movie I've seen and really enjoyed. It's a fairly old one, but when I saw it in the movies' listing on TV, I decided to watch again.

It's a story of a woman in a little town who has basically made a name for herself as the Runaway Bride because every time she is set to get married, she never makes it down the aisle. Instead, she runs. I mean turns tail and bolts away like her life depends on it. News of this woman's fiascoes with weddings makes its way to Ike Graham, a reporter in a big city. He is not the most popular reporter with his female readers and needs a story to redeem his chauvinistic ways. His editor suggests

Graham cover Maggie's fourth wedding attempt in hopes of helping his reputation.

One of my favorite scenes in Runaway Bride occurs when Graham is consoling Maggie at her fourth engagement party after her family and friends have openly humiliated her with jokes of her not running at the wedding. Not only has the news media enjoyed the sensationalism of Maggie's cold feet at the altar, but her family has also found much amusement in Maggie's fear. So a bit of a family roast ensues at the engagement party for Maggie's most recent attempt down the aisle.

The jokes start out lighthearted and seeming to want to take the edge off for Maggie, but quickly the jokes go a little too far. The hurt and shame are clear on Maggie's face as the smile she wore to endure the jokes quickly turns to sadness and everyone being amused but Maggie. Graham quickly rushes to her rescue while her fiancé stands by and lets the insults continue to be hurled at Maggie. With wit and sarcasm, Graham silences the laughs with a few jokes of his own and whisks Maggie away so she can let the tears that had already formed in her eyes flow and regain her composure.

As the two are having this discussion about what just happened, Maggie insists she did not need Graham's rescuing, and Graham points out the dysfunction in what just happened with her family and a little of the dysfunction in her as much of the jokes bared a tinge of truth. The conversation turns into an intense argument. As Maggie is objecting the whole time to all Graham is saying, she is realizing he seems to know her in a way fiancé #4 did not. I like this scene because I think it's when Maggie got her first glance at who she was through Graham's eyes.

He knew things about her that she never openly stated to anyone or perhaps she did not realize them herself until Graham pointed them out. They simply came from his observations of her character. So when the time came for her to find out who she was for herself, she had a great place to start. She started her own business creating these eclectic lamps, a gift and a passion she kept hidden from all her fiancés, but Graham knew.

The pair eventually fall in love, but not without a crucial conflict. Maggie's able to tell Graham about himself, the good, the bad, and the ugly, and he does the same for her, so the two set out to get married. Of course you would think this time she's going to walk down the aisle. I mean this is Richard Gere. But lo and behold, she bolts again, leaving Graham chasing behind her on foot at top speed as she flees on a FedEx truck.

What happens next is what grasps my attention this second time around seeing the movie. Maggie begins a journey of finding out who she is. Another of my favorite scenes lasts just a couple of minutes, but it's so powerful. Maggie has plates of eggs made in several different ways as she tries to see which one SHE likes. In every relationship she has been in, she took on the likes of that man. If he liked scrambled eggs, she liked scrambled eggs. Someone asked her which eggs she liked, and she paused because she really didn't know. She became who she thought the men in her life wanted and liked whatever they liked. It's on this journey that Maggie needs to know who she is because now she has found true love but doesn't know why she still can't walk down the aisle. Here was this great guy but Maggie has now realized that the issue was not just the men in her life but she was her own issue. She didn't know who she was, so she shape-shifted into who she thought she needed to be.

How many of us can relate? How many times have we taken on the likes, dislikes, attitudes, and disposition of someone else because we didn't have a strong foundation in who we are, especially in relationships or marriage? Too often we go into relationships because we feel we need someone to make us complete rather than going in whole and knowing who we are.

Before going into my marriage, I had a great deal of insecurity. I had just begun a real inward look at who I was when I met my husband. I had just decided that it was going to be just me and God and I didn't even want to date unless God stamped my potential beau with His stamp of approval. I felt like I had that when I met my husband, but the journey of finding out who I was didn't end. In fact it became more intense as I spent a lot of time in prayer and in my Bible.

I was devoted to finding out who I was, what my purpose was, and how I was to go about fulfilling it. I thank God for my godmother because she was there to see my passion for knowing and doing better, and she took me under her wing to help me. We can simply find ourselves wondering from place to place, job to job looking for, as Michael W. Smith sang it, "our place in this world." From childhood to adolescence to adulthood, we are forming an identity, and there are all kinds of influences around us, helping us make that identity. Life changes, and as it changes, so do we.

Going into my marriage, I remember still being in that place of self-discovery. Does that ever really end? But I distinctly remember wanting to be the best wife and the best mom, so I looked at other successful marriages trying to find those examples. I was not really being who I was but emulating what I saw. What really needed to happen was I needed to get the keys from those couples to a successful marriage and then apply them to who I was and who my husband was, not copy them. Knowing who you are is hard enough given all the influences around us. Now add life experiences that change us, reshape us, and losing self can become so easy. Too often we think the titles we carry are our identity. From being a daughter, to being a mom, a wife or a girlfriend, a business owner or an employee, women take on these things as identities, but these identities are not who we are. It's our temperament, our character that make us who we really are, and therefore, give those titles life and we get those things from our Creator.

In the Runaway Bride, Maggie explains why she ran from the other grooms: "When I was walking down the aisle, I was walking toward someone who had no idea who I really was. But you, you knew the real me." When Graham replies, "Yes, I did," Maggie returns with "But I didn't." It's beautiful and even helpful to Maggie that Graham knows her so well. She realized that was her attraction to him. He saw her. Who she truly was didn't seem invisible to him. In fact it was the vulnerability of them both that allowed them to see into each other.

But Maggie really sees that the true value in Graham's discovery of who she was could only be realized if Maggie saw who she was, too. I liken it to everyone telling you how beautiful you are but no matter how many times you hear it, you see yourself as anything but beautiful. Until you believe you are beautiful, what anyone else sees or says is really of no consequence. This was Maggie's issue and the issue for many of us. We become effective human beings when we walk confidently and aware of who we are. I empathize with Maggie because I found myself in that same place of having great loving people in my life who saw the real me and still loved me. But I didn't love me. I didn't know me. So I set out to know and love myself.

Pay attention to who's around you. Your relationships can enhance your discovery of who you are becoming or hinder it. If we can't take our friends telling us where we are messing up in areas of life, then we don't want friends. We want people who will cosign our mess and not check us on it. That's not a real friend. If I'm messing up, then I want my friends to tell me, and I thank God for my friends who do. At the onset of the separation, there were friends who scattered. I mean completely disappeared. Then there were the few, and I do mean few, who stuck it out and did their best to get us through. During the entire process, there were people who stayed, stepped in, and stepped out. All had their part to play in helping me discover who I truly was and heal during the discovery.

It's an issue of needing to be in control when we don't allow people to come alongside us and help us in the journey of discovery. Who do we think we are fooling!? The people who really know us can see when something is going on or when we need help. The flip side is having the right people in your life to help you build your self-confidence in walking in new arenas or taking risks. Graham encouraged Maggie's creativity, and though she left him at the altar, I think that encouragement caused her to branch out and open her own store after they broke up.

Real friends plant seeds of support for which they may never see the harvest. Never take someone's support for granted. We have to encourage each other's journey of discovering who we are because the truth is it is an endless journey. We are constantly evolving and maturing, hopefully. Everyone can't be a part of the journey, but thank God and cherish the people who are alongside of us.

Of course, in the Runaway Bride, Maggie and Graham get back together. I thought the story could have ended well even if they didn't, but I digress. Maggie reveals she likes eggs benedict, and she doesn't even like big weddings. She spent time getting to know herself and finding out who she was aside from all the characteristics of others she had picked up. It's a beautiful transformation and healing of a codependent person becoming interdependent. She no longer needed someone to make her feel confident or loved. She was loving herself. I applaud her for running every time she was about to get married and knowing in her gut she couldn't do it. I applaud her for opening herself up to real love. But most importantly I applaud her for taking the time to find out who she was.

That is what this time during and after the divorce has been like for me. It has been a time of using what deeply hurt me, hurt that cannot be explained in words, and using it to make me better driven by my relationship with God and good friends.

I am hoping to challenge you in these next few pages and chapters to discover yourself and to love yourself. Whatever challenge or tragedy you have faced happened to you, but it is not who you are. You may see that statement repeated quite a bit to really drive home the point. Face the good things in you and the areas that need some development. Knowing your strengths builds courage to face your weaknesses. Be brave in finding out who you are.

You may not like everything you find, but not facing it won't make it any better, and it certainly won't make those things go away. Love yourself enough to want the best, whole, complete you. Discovering your true likes and dislikes can be fun and exciting. You may be surprised by how much your likes and dislikes can change with time and experience. When you discover and embrace you, you find that because the best of you is flowing naturally, the best of everything else in life will flow naturally. You will attract true genuine things as you confidently walk in who you genuinely are. It's the art of being authentic.

<u>Reflection</u>

Do you really know who you are beyond the experiences life has handed you? When you think about who you are, do you hear the voices of the people who have tried to define you? Are those voices positive or negative? When was the last time you asked God about what He has to say about you?

<u>Notes</u>

"Don't ever

let Them tell you you are

too broken to bloom"

— Nadia Hasan

2 DISCOVERY THROUGH PAIN

Divorce: *Webster's* defines it as "the action or an instant of dissolving an action, separation, severance, a divorce of the secular and spiritual." Reading this definition, I am reminded of the many levels of conflict and pain that I went through.

Reflecting back, it wasn't just a separation and severance of the marriage; there was a divorce of who I was and a way of life I became used to living. The Bible speaks of divorce in a scripture I know we are all familiar, Malachi 2:16:

For the LORD God of Israel says

That He hates divorce,

For it covers one's garment with violence,"

Says the LORD of hosts.

"Therefore take heed to your spirit, That you do not deal treacherously.

In the Hebrew, the word *divorce* means dismissal, divorcement and comes from a root word meaning to be cut off, to be cut down, to destroy, to take away, to permit to perish. All of these definitions seem accurate. Divorce is so much on so many, many levels. There are things happening in your relationship with your spouse, in your other relationships, and in you. If you have children, there are more things going on with them, especially depending on age levels. You are trying to explain and make sure the kids are okay while trying to take care of yourself—if you really get a chance to do that. Family comes in and either attempts to make things better or makes things dramatically worse. It is a time of so much mixed emotion, changes, and transition. I totally get why God hates it. I hated that time and the moments of enduring it, but after much time and healing, I look back and see how the pain of that season of suffering gave me a lot.

I spent a season in depression in 2009, praying to God and just really looking for answers. I was a full-time mom and worked from home as an online instructor while also working as an entrepreneur. I couldn't help enjoying my life taking care of my babies all day, but I still had a passion for creativity and helping others. I was able to do that as an instructor and a wedding planner. Both of these just seemed like gifts and talents that came easy to me, so life felt good on those three levels: mom, employee, and entrepreneur. But I was still frustrated at times and felt like something was missing. I wondered if I was missing something with my husband. I loved my husband immensely.

We had good times, laughing and being with our kids. No marriage is perfect, and neither of us was looking for perfection. We always wanted God to be the center and to be focused on Him while focusing on our marriage and each other. There was so much change over the 10 years we were together. Most of it was happening inside each of us. We talked about it as much as we could. We were active in church, and everything on the surface seemed fine. Inside of me though, I could feel something was changing, evolving.

We spent a lot of time praying and studying the Bible together and individually in the first few years of marriage. The busier we got, the more sporadic it was when would do this together. But we were always praying together for our family. I remember my husband and I went through a long period of time where we would not watch TV preaching. We wanted God to show us His word, make His word come alive for us. We did not want anyone else's revelation at that time. We wanted God to reveal Himself to us.

As a full-time mom, I had a lot of time to read and pray. Listening to worship music and even dancing before the Lord in the privacy of my home were normal activities for me. It was doing these moments between me and the Lord that He gave me a powerful message: "I never told you to lose who you are to be wife and mother." I wept. Nothing had been truer in my life. I was missing me, and I was trying to replace me with being a wife, mom, and business owner. This may sound silly and some may disagree, but I feel like those are just extensions of who we are. Before we have children or tie the knot, we have an identity.

It is a discovery that begins in adolescence and continues throughout our entire life. We grow and evolve, and adding extensions of us into being parents and spouses compounds our identity. It can be a recipe for the greatest seek and find puzzle ever. It is a myth to believe that you find yourself one time in life and never lose who you are. Just like we grow and evolve physically through ages of our life, we grow and evolve internally, too. We mature hopefully from one season of life to the next. Who we were in adolescence hopefully is not who we are in our twenties and thirties and hopefully not who we are in our forties and fifties. I know I am not who I was, and coming into my forties, I really feel and see the difference.

Throughout life, if we are fortunate enough, we stay on this path of discovery, but what do you do when the journey is on pause or you have lost your way to you? I had begun the discovery before I met my husband and was still on the journey during our marriage. Somehow, some way, the journey got thwarted. It was like everything came into my life and pushed me away from me. I could see her, me, being pushed further and further to the back of the crowd, the crowd of faces that was now filled with my husband, children, church, friends, and work. The crowd of faces just grew and grew, and way in the back I could see her, me reaching out to me. My face was in color like everybody else's face, but the longer she stayed back there, the grayer her face became.

Eventually she just disappeared. Every once in a while, I would see her face in the crowd trying to get my attention, but something or someone would quickly distract me, and she would fade away into the sea of faces again.

In the midst of this back and forth of playing lost and found with myself, I was trying to explain to my husband what was happening within me. But something was happening within him, too. It was obvious, but he was less vocal about it. Even my older children noticed the changes happening in him. Here we both were, going through internal changes which were normal for any human being, but we were unable to effectively communicate to each other what was happening.

Looking back, I see it was because we did not know ourselves and didn't know what was happening within us. I can say that we both were going through seasons of spiritual growth that had such a huge impact inside and an even greater impact outside. So there was this inner and outer tug of war between us in trying to manage what we were experiencing internally and being able to communicate that externally, and finally the rope snapped. My husband and I just couldn't get it together. We just couldn't get on the same page. It is rather interesting, but since we have been divorced, through a lot of time, healing, and prayer, we have become better at communicating, and I would even say we are friends. But it was a journey for both of us to get here.

Relationships at the height of the divorce were just not cutting it. They either left me drained or just didn't satisfy me. I began to realize the issues were not the people around me but just like within the thick of my marriage, the issue was me. I was changing, evolving. I began to realize the importance of knowing I am a child of God and loving myself for whom God made me. I needed to have a better concept of loving myself, but I could not really do that until I had a better understanding of God's love for me. So what did God loving me look like if my most significant relationships were failures and tragedies of dysfunction?

That was the question I had to answer. Because loving me was necessary. It was critical. If we don't know how to love ourselves, then we can't live out "love your neighbor as you love yourself." We live in a society that doesn't love thy neighborhood because it never mastered loving itself. So for me, learning how to love me was critical to walking in my purpose and truest form of self, which meant I needed to see, experience, and feel God's love for me.

My church had a marriage seminar, and I decided to go because eventually, someday I would marry again. I truly enjoyed this seminar. I walked away with so much that would later become keys to this journey of healing from my divorce and discovery of my true self. The one thing that I'll never forget, that became the **IT** in this journey, was learning how to receive God's love. After the weekend was over, I began to pray every morning "God, I receive your love." And I prayed that simple prayer until it began to manifest itself. I found myself reading my Bible in a whole new way. I found myself hearing from God throughout my day.

I secretly began to hide my new love affair with God. I say secretly because at this time in my life I needed it to be just Him and me. No one's opinion of what I should and shouldn't do with my life was needed. In fact, that was what had been hindering me. I had one friendship that I valued above all in this season, but I think it had come to an impasse, and there needed to be a major shift. The problem was every time I tried to step back, not to end the friendship but to take care of me, I was met with heavy opposition.

This became the case in other relationships as well. I didn't realize it until later, but I was trying to set boundaries, healthy boundaries, to help me be a better me. So rather than announcing my departure or repositioning, I did it in secret. Sometimes you can't announce the changes you need to make for your life; you just have to do it. Haven't you ever noticed that other people in your world will do the exact same thing and expect YOU to make the adjustment?

So I began having my great relationship with my God. I began to experience His love in ways I never had. He helped me to clear out all the toxicity of past and present relationships. The layers upon layers of who I had been told to be, of who I had adapted to be began to fall away. The real me, the genuine me was there under it all. She had been there all the time. Now she was stepping to the forefront. She had color and was no longer in black and white. She was stepping to the front without any resistance because all the things and people who were blocking her were either being removed or voluntarily stepping aside.

Love was the key, God's love. Real, unconditional, untainted love. We spend so much time looking for it that we don't realize all we have to do is receive it. It's the one thing we can't do without, yet we misunderstand it. We try to replace it, destroy it, destroy others in the name of it, use it, abuse it, and manipulate it. The list goes on, but in all we do to it, the one thing we miss doing to it is simply receiving it. There's only one love that is complete, missing nothing, encompassing all that we could ever want or need and that's God's love. It is what we are created from and created to be.

God is love. It was His love for us that caused Him to create not just man but also woman so the two could have each other for fellowship and covenant. It may be a deep thought, but it's the reality of our creation and the reason many of us search for companionship thinking it will fill the void of love, and ultimately it's this backwards search that has left the human condition broken.

We don't search relationships to find love. We have relationships to be loved, to give love that's already in us. No one can love us and fill those empty places like God can. There really are some things only He can do. It's His perfect love that heals the broken places. It's His love that is the source of wholeness, and if we could find ourselves operating effectively in that love, wholeness could be a permanent state and not the journey being sought after the breaking. But that's just not the case. In fact it is in the breaking that we are pushed to the realization of the magnitude and availability of love.

It's the breaking that causes the empty places that can now have the toxins replaced and filled with that perfect love. It's a love given to us because we are worthy and worth dying for ultimately. The secret, which isn't a secret, is He wants to love us. The love is available. Just open yourself to receive it. I say this to inform for some and remind for others that everything you've been looking to find about love is real.

It's why you can forgive. Because you know what it's like to be forgiven. It's why you can see the hurting. Because you know what it's like to hurt and not be seen. It's why you so generously give because you have been filled by the most generous of them all. Too many of us go from relationship to relationship either broken or doing the breaking because 1) we don't know what it means to love unconditionally and that's because 2) we've never really learned to love ourselves. If you really loved yourself, you would know how to treat yourself and ultimately treat others.

Loving yourself begins with receiving His love. It's where identity is found. So my quest is to simply say every day, "Love, come and fill me." I want love to overflow from me, never leak. Leaking loves means I'm not being filled and let's be real. People fail us every day. Our expectations are too high for some and too low for others. Either way, we all have expectations of love that the human condition cannot always meet.

So in order to walk effectively and efficiently in love, we must first be filled then share it and then be filled again. Repeat often, never skipping a step. To those who really understand what it's like to want to be whole and have had a glimpse of wholeness only to be broken again, you know this quest to be filled by the ultimate in perfect love is necessary. It's life or death. So make the choice to open yourself up to being filled again. Trust Him with your heart. He can be trusted. The war is over. Love won and you're the prize.

<u>Reflection</u>

I am saving this reflection for after the next section. Here you can note any takeaway thoughts you got from this chapter. Pain is a serious topic to reflect on, and we are not done with it.

<u>Notes</u>

"Pain insists upon being attended to. God whispers to us in our pleasures, speaks in our consciences, but shouts in our pains. It is his megaphone to rouse a deaf world."

— C.S. Lewis

3 PAIN HAS A VOICE

The pain we experience throughout life has a voice. Our problem is we try to silence or ignore the voice of pain. But if we let the pain speak, we can not only find our healing, but also learn how to never endure that pain again.

So there I was, lying in bed, thinking about "it": my pain and what that pain had done to me. Then I began to think of what the pain had done FOR me. How it pushed me further in my walk with God and how I was doing more than finding myself but redefining myself. I was becoming someone new, someone stronger, someone BRAVER. My pain was talking to me, and I was listening.

I grabbed my phone and began to make notes about this dialogue I was having with my pain. You see, giving it a voice also gave it freedom. I was releasing it instead of self-medicating and putting Band-Aids on it! I was allowing it to teach me, release me, and release itself. You have to feel the pain. My daughter went through surgery at ten years old. She had a septic hip, and the fix was to have a surgeon go in and release the fluid before the toxins destroyed the rest of her joints, leaving her open to arthritis later in life. Thinking about my daughter's experience opened up a whole new window of understanding of how important it is to release the toxins before they destroy other parts of our lives, rendering us vulnerable to other issues down the road of life.

After the surgery, she was in pain, but it was a different pain. She was feeling the effects of having been cut open, but it wasn't the same pain as when the fluid was still on her hip. Nevertheless, the only thing my then 9-year-old baby knew was her hip had caused her excruciating pain, and she was not going to step on that side. She wouldn't go to the bathroom; she wouldn't sit up. She wouldn't do anything.

Finally, we had to talk to her and explain that the doctors

went into her hip and took the nasty stuff out that was causing her pain, and it was okay to walk on the leg again. That's what the love of God does for us. It cuts away the dead and toxic things and leaves us ready for a road to recovery and restoration. She had associated the pain she felt before the surgery with the pain she was feeling now and just knew putting any pressure on that hip meant feeling that really bad pain. She finally decided to step on the leg, and there was pain but not like she felt before. This was the pain of surgery that led to her feeling better. If you could've seen the look on her face, it was an "Oh, it's not that bad" look.

So through the next few weeks and months, she would transition through the pain using a walker and undergoing physical therapy to be whole again. And that's what we have to do. We have to face the pain to realize that once God does the surgery, if we let Him, what we are now feeling is the pain from the surgery. This new pain of the unknown and uncertain future, also known as fear, assures us that if we stick with God's rehabilitation plan, we will be more than just fine. We will be as good as new.

When I was a little girl, 12 years old to be exact, I found out that my dad was really my step-dad. At first, I really didn't care too much. But it was an obvious source of pain for my mother. She was distraught that I even found out and was angry that a family member told me. She wanted that secret to stay buried. Once I knew, it changed so much. It changed how my mom treated me. She was so afraid that I was angry with her, but I wasn't. I honestly didn't care at that time. But the more of a big deal my mom created, the more I became curious, and for a while, I sought to find my biological father. I was perfectly happy with the dad I had.

He was the only dad I ever knew, and he was a great dad. This new truth did, however, change our relationship. It was the perfect example of not facing pain properly and giving it voice so everyone could heal. I was just a kid who had her world rocked, and my parents were not handling it well, so they couldn't help me handle it well either. Once I became an adult in my mid-20s, I would come to meet my biological father only to find I was missing nothing at all—which was my first reaction. I have lived a really decent life with the man I have always known as Dad, and at no time did I ever think of or see him any differently. It was a pain for my mom that was hard to face when she was pregnant with me and even harder to face once I knew the truth.

As I dealt with my divorce, I was taken back in time to my mom and how we handled the truth about my dad. My family would either overreact to situations like this or not react at all. So when the separation and divorce began, my parents did not react. They did not know how to react. They had not gone through divorce, and just like they didn't know how to really help me with the truth about my dad, they didn't know how to help with the truth about the divorce. I don't share that to say my parents were bad, not at all! I share this to say that when you don't properly handle pain, it will have a longer effect on you and those around you, and the effect is never really good.

Yes, "it" hurt and probably still does because you won't face it. But as we do the work within, building ourselves back up, getting around the right people, we can take a step and see the pain as a purpose. As time goes on and we work through the pain, giving it a voice and not denying it, we give it and ourselves freedom. We find healing and wholeness. As an added bonus, you can now help others give their pain a voice and find healing and wholeness. You find a desire to see others live the restored life you are now living. Not to mention, you develop a boldness and a tenacity that won't allow anything to take you backwards from the place where you've found your voice, your passion, your healing.

Pain and Purpose

In the past couple of years, I have done a lot of reflecting and found I'm really grateful for the life I have and even for the struggles of my life. I would say one of life's greatest lessons has been there's purpose in the pain. I think about childbirth and having had my own children; I think about my mom and the labor pains she experienced getting me here. My coming to be in this world was anything but a fairy tale, but I'm grateful to my mom because there was purpose in the pain she went through to get me here. That purpose lives in me. It's hard to see any purpose when we are in pain of any kind. But there really is. Sitting here thinking about my mom's labor to get me here and my last three years on this planet, I've discovered a few lessons about pain.

First, the pain teaches you your capacity. When you can look back and see what you've survived, you get a great glimpse of your capacity to endure and that capacity increases because of the strength God gives you to endure.

The pain also exemplifies the grace of God in and on your

life. In labor, the female body does some amazing things. The birthing process causes things to stretch really big. But after the baby has safely entered the world, the body is restored to a somewhat normal state. There are physical signs that labor happened, but eventually we are restored to walking and moving again. That's how grace restores us. Sure there maybe scars, but we can be healed and go on.

Another lesson about the pain is it teaches you your source. I remember my own labor pains, and I'm sure my mom would agree that there were moments you call on God and I did! But the pain of life will teach you to run to God first, only to find He's right there with you. He is our source of strength, healing, joy, and love through the pain.

A greater point about pain is it wasn't just for you. I have been able to relate to so many women who have been through or are going through the very painful life events I've survived. We were never meant to do life alone. There's power in unity and community. We are to show this world there is hope and that Jesus is that hope. Sharing your story and how God got you through will help someone else. Take my word for it.

What doesn't kill you can make you stronger if you let it. A lot of the things in my life aren't what I want them to be, but when I don't dwell on that, I can really see what God has done and is doing through me. I choose to be happy and enjoy life even though there are moments when I still fight with life's pain. I have so much to be thankful for as I look around me. Best of all I get to open my heart every day to receive and then give God's love to this world. Don't let the pain make you bitter and steal your life from you. Let the pain show who God is and who He made you to be. Find your purpose in the pain and then go help someone discover his or hers.

<u>Reflection</u>

This is probably the most challenging of the chapters because you have to look at your pain and find the purpose or how it led you to your purpose. I never saw myself writing a book until I realized I had something to say. Take inventory of your pain.

<u>Notes</u>

"**Habit is habit, and not to be flung out of the window by any man, but coaxed down-stairs one step at a time.**"
— Mark Twain

4 RECOVERING ALONG THE JOURNEY

I always wanted to be a workout fanatic and have had my moments over my life where I would try to get in some kind of activity. I have walked trails for a season. I took tennis lessons for a summer. I even took ballroom dance lessons for a season to get fit and shed a few pounds. At the height of my separation and divorce, I lost a very large amount of weight rather quickly. It was a dramatic change. I must say it was one of those "everything works to the good of them who love the Lord" moments. Losing weight through stress was never the desire or goal, but it worked to my benefit, and I was two clothes sizes smaller in a matter of weeks.

It was then that I went back to trying to work out, but this time my goal was not to lose weight but tone and strengthen my muscles. We all have muscles. They are just tighter and more developed for some of us than for others. They are a part of our physical makeup, and they are important. We use some muscles in everyday movement and then others have to be worked out or developed with a little more intent and effort. Muscles that are not used will waste away, and it happens rather quickly. Maintaining muscle is just as important as building it and requires being just as intentional.

I think the same is true with the muscles in our personalities, our inner strengths and abilities. We can lose our confidence when we don't properly exercise those muscles. Walking in our strengths, those things we do naturally, helps to build our personality and character muscles. Sometimes life causes us to put our natural gifts and talents on pause, especially those gifts and talents directly tied to who we are.

It could be new career moves, new relationships, new babies, death, and pretty much anything can cause us to put who we naturally are on pause. What we may not realize is we need those muscles. We need those gifts and talents that come so naturally to help us discover and/or maintain who we are. The great thing is you can get that muscle tone back. What's even greater is no matter what curve balls life throws you, what's in you can never be denied. In fact seasons of transition and what looks like bad choices can be the best gym to train and develop those muscles. God uses all things for our good. You will answer the call within you at the proper time of releasing those gifts and talents because that call just does not go away. But we have a part to play.

The first place I find myself in any of the seasons of transition that have occurred in my life is facing my current reality. One of the realities I had to face and I think many of us want to ignore or even pretend is not real is that we are hurt and not okay. Going back to the gym analogy, it is usually clothes fitting differently or seeing ourselves in the mirror that cause to us to take note of the need to consider adding some cardio or a workout routine to our life. Facing the reality of being in a state of hurt or confusion or even depression is the first step to recovery.

Once we are willing to look at where we are and be honest with ourselves, we can take the next step in planning a program of recovery. It will involve honesty, some self-work, and bringing the right people alongside of you to assist in the recovery program. I would not be where I am today if it were not for my close family and friends and my church of which I can include in those I consider family and friends. There is no way I can leave God out of this equation for me, just no way and He uses people to help us.

I learned that it's okay to not be okay. What's not okay is to suffer in silence and never reach out for help. I know I have had my share of those days. I fought depression A LOT as a teenager and into my early twenties. It would lift its ugly head periodically throughout my thirties. Add the pain and uncertainty of divorce and depression seems unavoidable. But over the past six years, I have learned the power of saying "I am not okay."

The challenge has been in deciding whom I say that to because more damage can be done if that statement falls on the wrong ears or in the wrong hands. It's true that hurt people hurt people. It is also true that healed people heal people. Life has taught me the power of honesty and vulnerability. They can be good and bad when they fall into the wrong hands. We have to guard our hearts during these times by talking to the right people and at the same time leave room in our hearts to receive the love and support we need.

I spent time with therapists and sought Godly counsel at key times in my life. During and after the divorce were definitely times to do it. My pastor Steve Kelly says, "Never waste a challenge." Looking back at every time my heart was broken, I was disappointed, or let myself down through my own choices; these were moments that drew me closer to God and ultimately closer to myself. It will be a running theme throughout my life, the closer I get to God, the closer I get to who I am at my core.

Depression for me became a fight to mature my responses to pain and disappointment. We cannot avoid these things. As long as we are in this world dealing with other humans, we will face failures and mistakes. It is our response to them that will determine whether win or lose, whether we rise or fall, or whether we move forward or stay stuck. To me if you learn from your past mistakes and disappointments, then you win. We can never lose when we learn to grow who we are on the inside to have a better response on the outside.

The first step is admission. It's okay to not be okay. Some of us independent people can be our own worst enemy. Time has taught me how to face the pain, the negative thoughts, and emotional floods and find the right kind of help. Today I have found solace in my relationship with God and in prayer.

Understand there is healing power in human touch and connection, too. So whether you get help in prayer or from talking to someone, THERE IS HELP!

It's okay to not be okay. You don't have to pretend, and don't let people who can't understand your pain "church talk" you into hiding the pain because they think you should be over it "by now." If you need help, you need help. Please reach out to a professional counselor, a friend, and foremost God. I do get that sometimes talking to God may not seem like enough, but He is there, and if you listen, He will point you into that safe place to get help.

It's okay to not be okay. We live in a society where we can mask our pain in Facebook statuses, clever tweets, and phony smiles around friends and loved ones. But at the end of the day, when we get home and we are alone with ourselves, the reality of the pain will punch us right in the face. Understand that you are not alone. I have been there. It's hard to see it when you're in it, but the pain has purpose. It is not the end of your life. This is only a page in the story. You'll get through it. Don't quit.

You can live and live better than ever before.

First, do the work on the inside. It was during the times of true inner healing and self-development that I caught glimpses of some of my natural gifts and abilities. Life doesn't always give us a time out. So often we are still working at our jobs or developing that new business while other things are going on in our life. Challenging times are perfect for perspective adjustment and character training.

As I went through those challenging seasons and events like my divorce, God was giving me all the tools I needed to get a better perspective on life and discover some of the things I was really good at doing. One of things I discovered at the end of a potential dating situation was I had a heart for people and helping others. Seems strange to realize that then, but I needed to know why things ended the way they did and what did that experience teach me. Sure there are lots of negatives you can walk away with, but God wanted me to see the positives because He would later use those things in me to help others and expand my horizons.

Next, stop ignoring the call. There are always signs when we need to either start working out or get back into working. Some signs are subtler than others, but we all know when we need to step it up. The same is true when it comes to working and building up our character. You can sense the changes within you. Some things you used to like you don't like anymore. Things that were once funny aren't funny to you anymore. Frustrations escalate, and it seems like there's something wrong with everyone around you. But it is you that is the issue. You're growing. You're evolving. You're changing. The only problem is you are running from the call to get into the self-discovery gym and find out what's different. The more you ignore that passion within you to face you, the weaker the muscle will get until you get back into the gym.

Third, check your circle. Are the people around you inspiring you to return to that call? Are they encouraging you on your journey of self-discovery and self-development or fighting against the change happening inside of you? The first thing you may notice when you change and grow is that your circle changes. Friends will either fall off or draw closer to you, but there will be a shift, and this is not a negative thing always. It can seem like it. Who wants to lose people? But we have to remember that not everyone is meant to go the distance in our journey. Some for a season, some for a reason, and some for a lifetime, that's just the way it is. We all need support and encouragement just as much as we should give it. Be sure you have people around you who won't let you give up on you.

Sometimes you have to get out from where you are to remember where you are supposed to be going. Do I mean go on a trip? Not necessarily, but you sometimes need to get out of comfortable surroundings to be pushed into moving forward. I'm sure you've heard of muscles plateauing. Basically you have hit a point where the muscle is no longer being challenged. You're going to have to get out from where you are, momentarily perhaps, to see that you are not doing enough to work that muscle of greatness inside of you.

And finally, see beyond yourself. Sometimes the best way to build you up is to celebrate someone else. Seeing others excel or achieve greatness and celebrating with them is one of the best sources of inspiration to push you into taking steps to achieve YOUR next level of greatness. I love LOVE! And seeing others find it either through self-discovery or relationships really excites me. It gives me hope in the relationships I will build and motivation to continue to cultivate the relationships I have. The ending of my marriage by no means made me bitter with love. Absolutely not! In fact, it was God's love that gave me the courage to love myself more and fight for myself. God loved me before my marriage, during, and after it ended. So being able to celebrate love for myself and with others inspires me to continue to love on whole new levels.

Life is an endless journey in self-discovery. The challenge I think is to understand self, who you are at your core, not the labels and titles you have picked up over the years. When you lose who you are, you become who you are with. Maybe you grew up around emotional abuse and didn't realize it. Insecurity strikes us all in those formidable years of childhood and adolescence.

There are seasons of life where we fight insecurity and trying to live out who God is telling us we are in an environment that tells us anything but. Something I have noticed in my own journey of self-discovery is my personal progression would be directly related to the progression of the world around me. As I was growing inside, so was my world outside. Whether it was in relationships or opportunities, my world would expand and grow. But there was always something trying to thwart the process, never fail!

It's in our most spiritually transitional periods in life where it seems like all hell will come against us to stop that discovery, but the work is worth it. That discovery of who you are at your core brings an amazing freedom. It brings CLARITY. You can learn so much about yourself in those seasons, good and bad. You realize your worth.

I highly recommend you read *Boundaries: When to Say Yes, How to Say No to Take Control of Your Life* by Drs. Henry Cloud and John Townsend. It will change your life! If you've never had healthy boundaries, you will. I've been told to read this book more times than I want to say. I finally sat my happy hips down to read it and wow!

It is all about boundary myths, the need for boundaries, and how to build healthy boundaries. Healthy boundaries means having a "no" and a "yes" that allow you to know who and what you are responsible for and who and what you are not responsible for. In other words, every issue is not your issue to take on in your life. Every person is not for you to help. Jesus is the only person who can save and even He had healthy boundaries in His ministry. Weak boundaries lead to emotional abuse and codependency.

The thing I discovered about me was I was a people pleaser, which made me codependent to people with selfish personality disorders, such as passive aggressive and narcissists. As a people pleaser, having weak boundaries made me a victim and a victimizer of people with these personality orders because I could and would take on their personality traits. These weak boundaries become alluring to these personality disorders. Although helping people is who I am and is God's nature inherent in me, I was using this gift to my detriment. My desire to help could quickly become a need to please when I got stuck in the cyclical behavior of someone who didn't respect my boundaries. In other words, at my weakest moments, the kindness of my heart was taking advantage of because I did not have healthy boundaries.

Since I discovered my issue was people pleasing, I've found the beauty of interdependence. It's when you have a healthy balance of give and take in life. There are great relationships feeding into you as you are giving to them. It's enjoying being alone but not feeling lonely. It's building good relationships and setting boundaries with people who may not be the best for you but you don't want to cut them off. It's about respecting others' "no" and having respects for your own "no."

There is nothing wrong with saying "yes," but it may not always be possible or a good idea to yes. Do you have healthy boundaries? Boundaries can be unhealthy. Do you know what healthy boundaries look like? Get the book! You'll thank me later.

We are all a work in progress, and progress takes work. Your process needs to show progress, so get to work. Do your part to build your muscles up. Find great workout partners so you can encourage each other in your natural gifts and talents. Help each other see the great things. I am talking about genuine accountability that supports strengths AND weaknesses. We are not supposed to do this life alone.

The journey of self-discovery will find you in places where you either revive a dream you were already given or birth a new dream. But it is in the process that these dreams are even revealed. Don't be afraid to continue on this journey even as you find out the not so great things about yourself. Working out hurts at first, but as you move past the pain, muscles develop and strength comes. Stay the course.

<u>Reflection</u>

If you or someone you know is in a season of recovery, I suggest taking inventory of what that looks like for you based on the things discussed in this chapter. Knowing where you are in the self-discovery journey helps you find your way closer to your next destination. You cannot move to the next place until you have conquered this place.

<u>Notes</u>

THE ART OF FRIENDSHIP

"Friendship is unnecessary, like philosophy, like art.... It has no survival value; rather it is one of those things which give value to survival."

-C. S. Lewis

"There are no goodbyes for us. Wherever you are, you
will always be in my heart."
- Mahatma Gandhi -

5 AND THEN THERE WAS ONE

I want to share some thoughts specific to divorce. Please
don't tune out or skip this section if divorce does apply to you. I
am hoping to inspire those who have faced divorce to move
into a new way of thinking about what happened with some of
the major relationships in their world. I am also hoping to give
some insight to those who may have friends or family who are
facing divorce or have been through divorce but cannot relate
to the experience.

Hopefully you gain some insight into how you can help those
people through this critical and painful experience or at least
come to understand a glimpse of what is happening in their
world. Though all of our experiences will be different, one of
the aspects of divorce that was most challenging and that many

of us go through is the dispersing, division, and/or disappearance of friends and family. There are so many feelings and thoughts that happen when the reality that you are getting divorced kicks in to your mindset. "What will my friends and family think and say" is one of them. It almost seems like you need to send out a press release or call a news conference to dispel the rumors or combat the lies. There are always two sides to every story, but then there is the truth. When you are going through this hurricane of a life event, friends' and family's reactions are rather important. You want the support and you want relationships to continue, but here's the truth: things will be different, and there's not much you can do about it except choose how you will respond.

Some will choose sides. Some will treat you like you are a plague because they think the "spirit of divorce" will get on their marriage. (These are the super religious dummies.) Then you will have those who will stand by from beginning to end, which for some will be a great number and for others will be less than a handful. And anyone who has been through divorce knows what you are about to face and may be the best support—if they have healed and are healthy themselves.

The key is to not really over concern yourself with this

scattering. That is a challenge, I know, but I want everyone who is facing divorce or just on the other side to try to keep this thought in mind. Get yourself into counseling and create a support system that is going to get you through this. You can't control people, and as much as we say we don't care what people think, this is a time where you are not in your best frame of mind, and your emotions can easily be swayed. Now is the time that you must make yourself and your immediate family, especially children, top priority in getting help and support to get through this.

At one point it felt like I was the only person on this planet. I had friends who wanted me to console THEM while I was going through hell. I had friends who took the snob road. I had family who took his side not even knowing the story but was of the mindset that no matter what is happening, no matter how unhappy you are, even if you are in harm's way, you don't divorce.

As I stated in the beginning, I am not a proponent of divorce. If you can avoid it, please do so. I understood where these people were coming from in a way. Keep in mind, none of these people who felt this way had successful marriages that stood as proof that this mentality was good. But the onslaught of people I barely knew now inserting themselves into my life and the mass exodus of people I had known for years left me feeling like the only person on the planet. I did eventually see that I had a support system. It was small in number, but quantity is no indicator of quality in situations like this. And therapy was a great help! Therapy provided a place of safety because there was no bias. They did not know him or me, so they were able to objectively give me insight to help me and my kids. You'll need that place to freely vent and then in turn receive some good advice and counsel.

Then there was church. I am very open in everything I write about how important God is to me, and His relationship is the one that started me on this journey and ultimately got me through it. It was in the messages I heard and the people who came alongside me, who helped me get through the divorce. There were times it seemed like God was targeting me and my heart. He was after any seed of bitterness, pain, or self-loathing. My pastor would preach on relationships, forgiveness, or knowing if you're growing and I mean whole sermon series.

It felt like God was determined to not let this experience destroy me but mature me and get me on the path of reaching my destiny. Looking back, I realized I had a true destination

God wanted me to reach, and the entire universe was conspiring to get me there. He had my attention, and my heart was open to correction, healing, and restoration. We, God and I, were putting in the work. If you are fortunate enough to have a good, sound friend or family member who has survived divorce, and then coupled with a counselor or therapist and your loved ones committed to being there for you, you have a good support system to survive. You will need it.

The biggest thing I walked away from during this aspect of the process was that what I was seeing was relative to what I was feeling, which is why emotions can be such a bad judge of perspective. On the other side, the better side of the divorce process, I was able to see that though some friends and family did walk away from me, not all did. Some just didn't know what to do or how to handle it. They loved us both but just didn't know how to help. Experience is sometimes the best teacher. So the best advice and the best sounding boards came from those who had been through what I was now facing. Even then, some of the greatest moments of discovery and perspective shift came as I looked inward and continued looking into myself.

One of my purposes in writing this book was to reveal that God had really put a passion in me to dispel some myths and flat out lies about this journey. Some of the people who deserted me helped to perpetuate those myths and lies. There was one group that often gave me the most problems: the super religious people. Yes, God does hate divorce, but God does NOT hate the divorcees. He hates divorce because of what it does to the individuals and the family unit. Divorce is not the answer to family problems, but if you're in something that is ultimately not healthy mentally or physically or both, then divorce may be the end result. God, family and friends, and sound counseling will be critical. Key word is "sound." Sometimes counsel needs to come from a professional that does not know the both of you. I know this is repetitive and critically important to grasping what is happening.

By the time the dust had settled and life began to find some sense of order, a great deal of clarity showed up. It started with my relationship with God and cultivated with my relationship with myself. Having these two relationships grow and give me a greater sense of worth and purpose opened my eyes to what marriage should look like and how it would work best for me when I did it again. I found a better insight into how to manage relationship issues because of what I was dealing with inside myself and how that was affecting the relationships around me. Hindsight is indeed 20/20. Had I known some of the things I know now, maybe my marriage would have survived. But then maybe things had to fall apart so they could come together better than ever before. The real answer to relationship problems within a marriage lies in education of what marriage is and what marriage is not. It lies in creating two individually whole people who enter marriage relatively healthy and not looking to their partner to complete them but to complement them. We are only completed in the love of Christ. That completion allows us to love ourselves and therefore have a healthy outlook into a mate with realistic expectations.

Being comfortable with whom you are and trusting yourself allows you to understand how trust really works with people. The Bible states "It is better to take refuge in the Lord than to trust in people" (Psalms 118:8, NLT). Yet we know that we were created for relationship, and God made the woman so Adam would have someone of his own kind to relate. "The Lord said it is not good for the man to be alone. I will make him a helper suitable for him" (Genesis 2:28, NLT). People cannot be the answer to everything we need in life. They have a part to play for sure, but we cannot place unrealistic expectations on the people in our world. Be good with being alone though you don't have to want to be alone forever and always. If you can't stand to be alone with yourself, no one else will be comfortable with being alone with you either. News flash: you are NOT who you were when this process started, and if you are just starting the process, you will not be the same once the process is complete. Let me be clear. There is more than just a divorce process happening here; there's another process and that is rebuilding and redefining who you are. You are not the divorce. The divorce does not define you. It is what happened to you, but it is not who you are.

<u>Reflection</u>

How can you as a friend, see beyond yourself and help someone who may be facing something you have overcome? How can you as an individual find a way to deal with the inner turmoil and not have it affect your relationships? That is a big and challenging question, but it is necessary. It will make a world of a difference in your life.

<u>Notes</u>

"I am not afraid of storms for I am learning how to sail my ship."

-Louisa May Alcott

6 THE PERFECT STORM

A perfect storm is defined as "a storm arising from a rare combination of adverse meteorological factors" dictionary.com). In the movie *The Day After Tomorrow*, a series of different weather events send the world into a new ice age. One weather event triggers several others, and by the time it's discovered, there's a major freeze taking over, and it becomes a race against time to save friends and loved ones.

The Perfect Storm is another movie that follows a similar storyline. In the movie, a confluence of weather conditions again creates one major storm, but the action takes place in the ocean and leaves for a rather hair-raising plot. These movies and the idea of the perfect storm came back to me as I have been talking with friends and reflecting on our human condition and how we relate to each other.

One of my friends told me they always seemed to feel at odds with their significant other. But it really wasn't about being at odds with one another. There was nothing wrong with them as a collective unit. Individually, however, they were both working through personal issues that affected how they related to each other. Because they couldn't deal with individual issues, they could not see that her hurricane and his tornado were forming the perfect storm—adverse weather conditions in two different areas converging into one major storm.

We all go through storms. It doesn't have to be a romantic relationship. It can be with our children, siblings, friends, co-workers that internal conflicts are unintentionally causing external conflicts. But I think what we miss is that we can be going through individual storms and have them all converge into this perfect storm and not realize it. Ever have those moments where you stop and say, "What is wrong with her!?" Because the behavior is either out of character for her or you have become more sensitive to how you are communicating with her. Your lightning might be affecting me, and my floodwaters could be affecting you, and we just never stop and think that the behavior may have absolutely nothing to do with us as individuals but everything to do with the individual displaying the behavior. In other words, it *ain't* always about you.

What I began to see for myself was the ability to look beyond myself and into that person to see there was something going on that had nothing to do with me. I remember during the divorce there were friends who just disappeared. I felt really abandoned, like I had this disease called Divorce and no one wanted to catch it. Then to add the rumors and lies from people who assumed they knew what was going on, nothing about friendship or even family for that matter felt loving in this season.

Now that I have come to a place of clarity and soundness of mind, I can look back and see that a lot of my friends had things going on in their lives. Then there were friends who just needed to go because they were crazy. No other way I can really put it. They loved drama, so if they didn't have any of their own, they would get into yours and even make it about them. Crazy. But I am grateful that I can look back and see that with clarity because now I am able to have more grace for people realizing that they need more prayers for their behavior and not my judgment.

Another definition of a perfect storm is "a particularly bad or critical state of affairs, arising from a number of negative and unpredictable factors" (dictionary.com).

What if there's nothing wrong with your relationships, per se, except the inability to see the other person's clouds because you can't see past your own? It's hard to see what challenges someone else could be facing when you are dealing with your own. And it doesn't have to be major challenges. It could just be a season of self-awareness or growth that has an extrovert acting like an introvert just because of what is happening within them. What if you made a permanent decision to end a business or personal relationship based on temporary feelings? I think this is why some relationships, regardless of type or level, survive major storms unless it is physically or emotionally abusive. They get past the personal storms and still maintain the relationship because they allow for growth and evolution within each other. You have to give people room to manage in their own storms while you manage yours and still be able to come back together to enjoy the sunshine again.

Wouldn't it be great if we could all walk around with

personal weather reports on our shirts on those days or seasons when we are in a storm?

Hurricane ... Tornado ... Partly Sunny ... Tsunami printed clearly on our chest so we could know what some of our friends, acquaintances, and family were going through. Could we be in a better position to help? Would we help? Would we speak to the storms in each other's lives? So many questions but the one thing I do know is there is purpose in every storm. So while you may be dealing with a hurricane in your life, and your friend is going through a tsunami, there is purpose for you individually that will at the right time be seen collectively **if** you allow it. It's the collective purpose that comes after what looks like the perfect storm. It takes unconditional love, forgiveness, grace, and maturity. I never thought I would go through the challenges or heartbreaks that I have endured, but I am grateful for them. They have taught me great lessons and made me better. Now I can take the wisdom I gained and help someone else.

I remember one of my former business clients now friend called me one Sunday and needed my undivided attention. Sensing the severity of the message, I agreed. She would share with me that she had decided to get divorced. We talked for hours. My first questions to her were all the questions you would ask to get someone to not choose divorce. I was very adamant on the journey of divorce, and it was not something to take lightly at all. It does a real number on you internally and externally. After she said she was sure, and she did have some pretty major reasons, she asked for my advice. I told her several things I had learned. One of them was to write. Get a journal and use it as a safe place to get "it," the entire experience, out of you and not let it build up in you on those moments you may not have an outlet. Well I never would have imagined that advice would cultivate into her writing a book about her divorce. Being on the other side of my storm, I had the clarity to help her through hers. But if she had come to me for advice during my storm, I cannot say the advice would have been sound or wise.

We don't see the results of a storm until after it passes. When the storm passes, we see the debris it left, the trees it uprooted, or the flood damage once the water recedes. But if we are not careful, we will also miss the rainbow, the birds eating the seeds that have been brought to the surface, the sun that shines again, or the cool breeze on a normally hot and humid day. It is learning the lessons and then seeing how that tough lesson brought your growth, maturity, and a better chance at a purpose-filled life as God intended for you. We will not always see our storms forming in our personal lives, so of course we may miss the perfect storm forming in our relationships around us. Can we see it? I think so. It requires looking beyond self and saying just like I can be going through a season of things being uprooted and floodwaters washing things away, so can the people around me. It requires having the grace with others we ourselves want to receive when we are facing life's storms. Is it possible? Sure.

But it just may not be likely, and I think that's still okay. Everyone will not write a book or even take the time to help someone walking through a similar experience. We all are not going to choose to help someone, and that is okay. But for those of us, who do make that choice, take that choice very seriously. You have taken part ownership in someone else's recovery.

When you can objectively step back and look at each person you know, you can see that we can be our own entire individual storm. Sure hindsight is 20/20, so we see better after the storm. It was the passing of my own storms that allowed me to reflect and write this. When you set yourself aside and focus on the individual you're engaging as they are sharing what's going on in their life, you see we are not so different in that at any given moment we can go from calm to storm mode simply by living life. Even within our own storms, we can still have grace with the people around us and try our best to avoid the perfect storm. But if you miss the warning signs and if your iPhone isn't sending you a loud alert at 3 a.m. to warn you, you can still salvage your relationships with simple forgiveness, mercy, and grace with each other.

You'll realize that some of your relationships, no matter the type or level, can be better after the storm passes. And that is really the other point that I want to drive home other than we all have storms: good can come from these storms that make our relationships better because we are better individually. As we get better, we see better and even the purpose for some of our relationships can become clearer. Good can come from the storms.

<u>Reflection</u>

Can you recognize your storms? Better yet, can you recognize what could be causing your storm? Once you have that knowledge, you have the power to make more choices that help you and ultimately those around you. You can now be the meteorologist for a friend, family member, or even a total stranger and help them maneuver their storm.

<u>Notes</u>

"We change our behavior when the pain of staying the same becomes greater than the pain of changing. Consequences give us the pain that motivates us to change."
— Henry Cloud

7 TIME TO SET BOUNDARIES

The journey of self-discovery will not only illuminate who you are and who you have been, it will also illuminate the people around you and the circles you find yourself. The journey opens your eyes and your perspective on your world. As I said earlier, divorce causes more than a divide in a relationship and/or a family but divides friendships. In the thick of it, divorce gives some things a distorted view mainly because of the pain and anguish. The scars it leaves cannot only be found on you, but also on your friends and relationships. As the healing process begins and wounds begin to scab over, you will have an opportunity to put existing people in the proper place in your life and figure out where new people belong. It is a process indeed. Trying to manage your own healing and still be open to your other relationships requires honesty on where you are, transparency when you need help, and strength to do the necessary things to take care of yourself and those in your world.

Now that the healing has begun or is complete, everything seems different, and that is because they are. You are different. Hopefully that *different* is for the better. Now that you have done all that work to heal and peel away the layers of what went wrong and what went right, you have a better version of you that needs to find her way. The first thing I noticed when the pain subsided was people in my world looked different to me. Some of their actions no longer were acceptable, and I began to get a better sense of the type of people I wanted close to me and the people I would no longer allow that intimate access.

I went from a state of being desperate for someone, anyone to a state of I'll walk this thing out alone with just God before I sell the value of who I am to the lowest bidder. It was not an issue of pride but of self-worth. So it was time to set boundaries with new people and establish boundaries with existing relationships. This takes work! It started with recognizing I had become a people pleaser and then taking my worth back and saying the only One I need to please is God. It took listening to and not ignoring warning signs and also trusting myself to see the good in the people who were meant to be close to me. We must remember that just because one or two hurt us, not everyone is out to hurt us. We cannot judge the good of our future by the pain of our past.

There is a message center in my car that tells me when my car needs servicing. Yellow-lighted messages are warnings, but red messages mean there's a major problem and I have to stop the car IMMEDIATELY. For a few days, I had been getting a yellow warning message. I have a really good knowledge of the basic maintenance for cars, so I knew I had some time for this issue. Well, what I knew was wrong. I thought the warning message said one thing when in fact it said something totally different! I wasn't paying attention. I was so busy and often distracted. I just needed the car to get me where I needed to go, and I would take care of the issue later, an excuse? Absolutely! I likened this to an experience I had during my discovery journey. I found out a disturbing truth.

Why disturbing? Because I knew, I knew the truth and ignored the warning signs and instead believed what was told to me. I asked all the right questions, knowing the answers, but I used to give 100% trust until I had reason not to give it anymore.

Now the warnings were flooding back to me and clicking into one of the best deceptive ruses I'd seen in a good minute. But the TRUTH always comes out. It will set you free, but it just might make you mad first. It was a major wake-up call to begin to trust myself and trust the God inside of me. God is just as vested in our protection as He is in our freedom. He does not set us free to live anyway we want, but to live freely in service to Him. The hardest thing to accept was that the truth was in me. God was warning me. The message center started sending yellow warnings that turned to red, but I ignored them. Coming out on the other side of the divorce, not only did I find healing from the pain of the divorce, but also I found healing from issues I had before I ever got married. Self-worth and value were two of the issues I needed to address. I had to learn to trust myself again.

We have to learn to trust ourselves.

Remember the book I mentioned earlier, *Boundaries: When to Say Yes, How to Say No to Take Control of Your Life*? The book I loved so much? Many years ago, someone very close to me recognized the people pleasing issue I had and recommended that book to me. I started reading the book, but because it was a slow build, I put it down. Little did I know, boundaries would come up again in my life, and the book would be recommended to me again. It is funny how other people can help you see the issues you need to address that you cannot readily see for yourself. I downloaded the newest version of *Boundaries* and started to read it again. At the time of starting the book, yet again, I was trying to recover from the pain of yet *another* betrayal just on the other side of my divorce. I purposefully set my mind to read this book. I let it get by me the first time, but not this time. I skipped the end of the first chapter and when I began to read the second chapter, which was getting to the heart of the book, I literally wanted to kick myself. I began to cry as I read because there it was. There *I* was. Everything I needed to know about managing this new life I was building and managing current and new relationships was within my reach all along.

I read…

"Boundaries define us. They define what is me and what is not me. A boundary shows me where I end and someone else begins, leading me to a sense of ownership. Knowing what I am to own and take responsibility for gives me freedom. Taking responsibility for my life opens up many different options. Boundaries help us keep the good in

and the bad out. Setting boundaries inevitably involves taking responsibility for your choices. You are the one who makes them. You are the one who must live with their consequences. And you are the one who may be keeping yourself from making the choices you could be happy with. We must own our own thoughts and clarify distorted thinking." —Henry Cloud

A great deal of this journey of self-discovery involved receiving God's love and realizing that I mattered. My mental and emotional health were important, and sometimes, keeping me healthy was going to mean setting boundaries with the people who would and would not have access to me. Here is a truth that not many of us are willing to accept: You carry something great inside of you. The God of the universe is not only madly in love with you, but He has placed a great love inside of you so you can be the love you were created to be. That won't always look as nice and sweet as it sounds.

When we begin to set boundaries with people we love, a really hard thing happens: they hurt. They may feel a hole where you used to plug up their aloneness, their disorganization, or their financial irresponsibility. Whatever it is, they will feel a loss. If you love them, this will be difficult for you to watch. But, when you are dealing with someone who is hurting, remember that your boundaries are both necessary for you and helpful for him or her. If you have been enabling them to be irresponsible, your limit setting may nudge them toward responsibility. -Henry Cloud

Cloud asserts a great point that helped me in my own walk through boundary setting: Setting boundaries is not just for your own benefit, but it can be for the benefit of the other person. I have experienced loss of people during this process, but I have also seen relationships go to new and better levels.

Sometimes we have people in positions they are not meant to be, and all we need to do is to reposition them. We will not always have to cut people lose or sever ties, but do not rule those actions out. Remember, setting healthy boundaries is about loving yourself and knowing where your responsibility starts and ends with your relationships. In Matthew 22:37-39, Jesus gives us the commandments we are to live by:

Jesus replied: "'Love the Lord your God with all your heart and with all your soul and with all your mind.' This is the first and greatest commandment. And the second is like it: 'Love your neighbor as yourself.' All the Law and the Prophets hang on these two commandments."

Before we can ever love others properly, we must know how to love ourselves. Before we can love ourselves, we must know or at least begin to grasp how much and how deeply God loves us. God's love helps us learn self-love, which helps us love others. If we are not properly loving ourselves or even accepting God's love for us, which He demonstrated through His Son, then we cannot properly love others. Boundaries allow us to embark on this key factor in self-discovery: God's love.

Once my boundaries were set, and I continued to allow God's love to transform and heal me, I found the strength and freedom to begin again. You know healing and confidence are within you when you can dream again and begin to step out again, taking chances and fulfilling the purpose of your life. It is possible to resurrect a dream and even dream a new and better one.

<u>Reflection</u>

Do you know you are a people pleaser and have no boundaries or unhealthy ones? Maybe you are not a people pleaser but just have a hard time with knowing what things are your responsibilities with the people in your world and what is not. I strongly suggest getting the book I mentioned in this chapter, but in the meantime, consider some ways you can begin to set boundaries for yourself. The first step is recognizing that you need them.

<u>Notes</u>

"I was made for more than being stuck in a vicious cycle of defeat. I am not made to be a victim of my poor choices. I was made to be a victorious child of God."

-Lysa TerKeurst

8 SIT IT OUT OR DANCE

Living near the beach, I have one of the most beautiful scenes of nature at my disposal, and I am guilty of not taking advantage of it as much as I would want to do so. One of my sacred romance moments, as I would like to call them, is heading to the beach for a sunrise. I have caught the sunrise by myself and with others, but no matter who is with me, no sunrise ever seems the same. What I love about the sunrise is it reminds me how much God is in control. Watching the waves crash and knowing that the earth is spinning as the sun makes its debut is amazing yet peaceful. The God who makes all this happen, who spoke this very world into existence, is the same God that made and loves me. He is the same God that made and loves you. I'll take a sunrise at 6 a.m. any time to start to my day!

It had been awhile since I shared the sunrise with anyone other than my daughters. I would invite people, but I guess 5:45 a.m. on a Saturday is a lot to ask, and I do understand. I also think that for a season I needed it to just be me and God. There was a lot of internal work that had to be done, and sometimes people can become distraction or even a crutch to keep us from the true work we need to do on ourselves. But along the journey of self-discovery and becoming whole, you will need people and times of refreshing.

I'm grateful that this one particular time a friend did say "yes" to an invitation to share a sunrise with me. I love sharing and to share such a beautiful piece of God's work with a friend was great. We had a great talk and got to relax. So much of the way we communicate today is through technology. Even when we are in each other's presence, we are still on our electronic devices rather than enjoying each other's company. It was good to have this moment to sit and communicate in person. It was very refreshing.

There's really nothing like spending time with someone and really listening to their story, hearing what's on their heart and even seeing the light on their face while they share. After seasons of self-work, it is good to get around great people and share life. That's the greatest to me. People matter. We all want to be heard. We all want to know we are not invisible. Sometimes it just takes the right person at the right time to listen and speak into our lives.

Relationships have the power to bring a refreshingly new view to your world. They have the power to heal. After you have lost relationships while maintaining some, you will have opportunities to develop new ones. In life we need people, not **a** person, but **people**. No one person can be everything to you and you can't be everything to someone else. Even Jesus, the son of God, had others to be there for Him to share. We are no exception.

In the book *Kitchen Table Wisdom*, author Rachel Naomi Remen, M.D. states,

"Listening is the oldest and perhaps the most powerful tool of healing. It is often through the quality of our listening and not the wisdom of our words that we are able to affect the most profound changes in the people around us. When we listen, we offer with our attention an opportunity for wholeness. Our listening creates sanctuary for the

homeless parts within the other person. That which has been denied,
unloved, devalued by themselves and others that which is hidden."

Relationships fall apart just like they fall together. Losing people can be hard, but it happens. Having the right response and remembering the greater good of the relationships you lose sets you up to gain new and better relationships. Your world can be expanding and that can be hard to see after a challenging season or a traumatic season where you have lost loved ones. Don't miss what God is doing in your world focusing on the wrong thing. Keep taking chances. Keep stepping out there. Keep being interruptible and letting new people into your world. All of these are a part of the journey.

Everything we learn about ourselves and those around us shapes the people we become. Relationships teach us about ourselves. Trace the seasons of growth in your life, and you will find two common threads: relationships ending and relationships beginning. That is because as you grow or mature, so should your relationships. There are those who grow with you on the journey, but you should realize that you will attract people who fit the season of your life that you're in, and you will find some relationships no longer fit into your life. It does not make them bad but you may have to readjust where these relationships fall on the priority list. We can love everyone but that does not mean that everyone should have equal access. I have found the strength and grace to let go of people who have to leave and welcome people who want to be a part of the continued journey. I can also give the consistent people the space they need in their lives as I take the space I need in mine. Someone very wise told me that the people in our lives do not belong to us. They belong to God. Trusting God with them is the best thing we can do for them.

New friendships and acquaintances can be a sign of life moving forward. Maybe you feel stuck and unsure. It's okay. We all go through that. But at some point, you have to decide that the season of pause to regain a sense of self has turned into a season of stuck. Choose to see what else life has to hold for you. It is not over. Life always gives us a chance to sit out or dance.

<u>Reflection</u>

In what ways do you relate well with people and what ways do you relate not so well? Are you missing out on new relationships because you have been focused on the old ones that are long gone? Is it time for a life reset and accept that moving forward is a choice?

<u>Notes</u>

THE ART OF MOVING
FORWARD

"God is the God of "right now." He doesn't want you sitting around regretting yesterday. Nor does He want you wringing your hands and worrying about the future. He wants you focusing on what He is saying to you and putting in front of you ... right now."

— Priscilla Shirer

"We must not confuse the command to love with the disease to please."
-Lysa TerKeurst

9 THANK GOD FOR "NO"

If life teaches us nothing else, it definitely teaches us that there will be times when God says "yes" and times when God says "no." Then there's my favorite response, "Wait." All of these responses are necessary because we have to learn to trust God when the plans are not clear, when the next step isn't revealed right away.

After a season of rebuilding life from the separation and divorce, I began to see where God had brought me from. Here I was with a seemingly stable job, my own place, my vehicle, my own life. He had really taught me that there were great abilities and gifts in me and one of them was resilience. I of course had my own plan for God for how He was going to restore my life. How many know how far that got me? He was even kind and merciful enough to let me live it for a little while. But there's this one prayer that I often pray that kind of gets me into what I call trouble. It's the "Not my will, but your will. Whatever you want me to do, wherever you want me to go, whatever you want me to say" prayer that has for as long as I can remember had a way of totally interrupting my life plan and implementing His. So like always, after praying that prayer, doors began to open, but then doors began to close.

It was the closing doors that brought some of the greatest pain and disappointment in that season. And when you've just survived a divorce, you think what in the world have I done to deserve this. But it isn't always that you've done something wrong. Maybe you're doing some things right. After time of course, you can see God's protection in the closed doors. You can see Him blocking things that were not a part of His plan for you. Jobs have ended after that prayer and relationships were severed. My absolute greatest lesson in one particular season is that loving someone should not hurt. I can remember moments of internal pain and anguish because I was trying to love something that wasn't real. It was not genuine on both sides. So rather than allowing myself to continue to hurt and be hurt, God cut it off.

"Enough," He said. I was so caught up in loving someone that I couldn't see how they didn't love me. They simply loved enjoyed receiving my love and my attention but wasn't remotely capable of giving it back on nowhere near the same level.

Your life often will only make sense in retrospect. Looking back at that time and that prayer, I realized that I did learn my capacity to give, forgive, and love based on my life source, my relationship with God. Because of His love for me, He began moving pieces in my life. We are meant to receive love in our relationships. "Being valued, cared for, adored and celebrated by another human being reinforces and strengthens our feelings of inner-security" (Shannon Tanner from *Worthy*).

Steven Furtick, pastor of Elevation Church in Charlotte, North Carolina, says never write people off, just keep a balance sheet. So I've been able to walk in love and healing and still set boundaries. When you've been deeply wounded, you can either learn from it or put steps into place to prevent it from happening again, or continue the cycles and the wounding. I took the steps toward prevention.

Divorce isn't the end of the world. It's not God's plan for our lives either, but if you find yourself facing divorce, know that you can recover. We all heal in different ways at different levels. Do what's best for you. Dedicate yourself to loving you and becoming whole again before you take on anything new. After my divorce, the last thing I needed was another relationship, especially one that would undo all the work God and I had just accomplished in my recovery. While I do believe that relationships aid in the healing process, the wrong relationships can damage you further and hinder the healing process. You have to really be intentional in who you let in your life. Vulnerability is a double-edged sword. It can be good and bad.

Your vulnerability in the wrong hands is dangerous! Two healing people can help each other heal, and they can also hurt each other further. Hurt people hurt people. But healed people heal people. When you've recovered from pain and hurt, you want to see others going through what you've been through receive the same wholeness you did. If you're truly healed, you won't hold anyone else back from their own healing and moving on with their life. I believe I had someone who wanted to see me healed but wasn't healed totally either. Good intentions with bad methods still equal wrong results.

When I began to find my own way and my own identity,

my vision changed. I saw my world differently. It was like I came to myself. That's when I saw myself evolving. My wants became clearer, and my desires changed. Understand that any doors God might close are because He either it is not the right time or He has something far better for you. Accepting the closed doors says you are ready for the one that is about to open. It is like wanting someone to fill your hands with a treasure, but your hands are full of trash. Empty your hands. Let it go. Accept that Father knows best and smile. That great and beautiful thing that is worthy of you is that much closer to finding you.

When you let go, you get through it. That is the point of all of this: you get through it. There is no real "how to" on navigating divorce because we are dealing with people, the most unpredictable, emotional, and fickle of God's creations. It would be interesting to see how animals handle divorce. But this book was designed to give some insight and hopefully some inspiration in getting through one of the most challenging and life-altering experiences ever. Like most traumatic experiences, its end result on and through you will come from a series of choices you have to make.

You won't always make the right choice because this isn't

going to always come down to right or wrong. Those words are left to the interpretation of those making the choices. That is to say what seems right in the moment could indeed be wrong in hindsight.

Looking back, there was so much I wish I could do over. There were so many decisions that at the time I thought were the right things to do, but looking back at the headspace I was in at given moments, the choice wasn't really the right choice. Through it all, I made it and like the song says, "I don't look like what I've been through." Being able to reflect on the past and smile speaks to clarity and wholeness.

Freedom can almost seem scary when you've been bound for so long. You have these moments when you taste what it's like to be free of inhibitions, worries, and the like, and it tastes great! But then you run back to the same place that you've been trying to escape. There's a psychological condition for this that is related to prisoners who have been incarcerated for so long that when they are freed, they wind up back in jail or prison because that is what's comfortable. And that's the problem: Comfortable!

So many times I've learned there's no growth in

comfortable, and it's pretty easy for me to step out in less challenging areas of life, those areas where I have the greatest confidence that stepping into the unknown will be rewarding, but what about the less confident areas? The areas that seem a little scary or vulnerable can be the very areas we need to step into because on the other side of that brave step is one thing we can be sure of, an opportunity to mature.

So take the step! Go beyond what's comfortable and don't look back unless you are reflecting on your growth. Choose not to stay stuck in a place of complacency or even pain. You can actually become used to being hurt and stay in that place. It's those unhealthy places that seek to stifle your vitality.

When I was a little girl, I developed a disdain for broccoli and seafood. My mother used to cook broccoli until it was an ugly green; I hated the smell and most of all the taste. I'll never forget once having to sit at the dinner table after my sisters had finished dinner because I would not eat my broccoli. I finally decided to stuff my mouth, trying to hide my gagging; show my parents the empty plate; and then run to the bathroom to spit it out. Yuck! My issue with seafood was not as bad, but I had an experience where the smell did not make me want to *taste*, but I was forced to eat it. I hated it. I don't know what I disliked most, the smell, the taste, or being forced to eat it. Nonetheless, they were experiences that made me steer clear of those two foods and honestly any food that did not smell good to me.

Well many years later, guess who now likes broccoli and even some seafood? I have always liked fresh (raw) broccoli, but I now can eat pretty, bright green broccoli and really enjoy it. I went to dinner with family recently and decided I would try some seafood, blackened flounder to be exact. I really enjoyed it. So what happened between childhood and now? I had my own guesses, but I did a little research on the good old World Wide Web.

There seems to be a lot of opinion in the world of nutrition that taste buds can be retrained though there are some who feel it is not possible. They also state that we lose taste buds as we get older. So retraining them is how new tastes are developed and old tastes are renewed. Given my experience, I would agree that your taste buds can indeed be retrained. Dare I say it, our taste can mature.

What if that is what maturity is all about, retraining? We don't grow new taste buds. In fact we lose thousands of them as we get older. What if the maturing in our taste can be compared to the maturing in our lives? Furtick says, "Don't mistake growth for maturity." In other words external growth or success should not be mistaken for inner maturity in character. Just as we don't grow new taste buds but retrain them, maybe our own true maturity comes from retraining our thoughts and actions regardless of past experiences and even childhood upbringing. There can be parts of life that we have been stuck in that could be retrained. We could learn to enjoy things we once disliked.

No matter your age, it's never too late.

Maybe you dislike reading and don't do it because you didn't like it when you were younger. Or maybe your dislike is a little more personal, like making new friends or finding a new relationship. Were you once sour to love because of a past or even recent experience? I say give it a go again. I will say that I found my new love for broccoli and flounder in a season of what I call "all things new." This has been a season of letting go of the old and even the current if it did not fit the path I was on for my future.

No more lamenting too long in seasons that you know are long over and the only thing stopping forward movement is you taking the step. Did those things, the broccoli or the fish, change? Not really. I think the change is within us. It's a newfound appreciation for life and a desire for the best adventures life has to offer. Even childhood experiences can be redeemed.

You never know what's out there if you never open yourself up to new experiences. I am a Disney movie fanatic. One of my favorite quotes from the movie *Up* is "Thanks for the adventure. Now go have another one." It's time to have a new adventure and retrain an old experience into a fresh and exciting new opportunity.

<u>Reflection</u>

In what ways have you grown that you may have overlooked? Maybe you never went through divorce. I never said this book was only for divorcees. Maybe you, like me, have been on this road of self-discovery and just haven't taken inventory of your growth. Do it! It is very encouraging and leads to your growing and maturing all the more for your purpose and this life's journey.

<u>Notes</u>

"Refuse to be average. Let your heart soar as high as it will."

— A.W. Tozer

10 NEW NORMAL

As I have gotten older, I have fallen in love with nature. I find myself watching the signs of the coming seasons. I love to notice the signs of seasons changing. Fall and spring are favorite seasons because the changes are so noticeable. With fall, the temperature drops on some nights. The days get shorter, thus it gets darker sooner. My favorite part of fall is watching the leaves change color and then fall to the ground. The seasons teach a great lesson. The seasons can teach us about patience and timing.

I haven't always been a fan of the word *patience*, but with age and experience, I do see its importance and need. *Trust*, another awesome word that we use rather flippantly, but when it comes to our lives and exercising patience, trust is key. What do we trust? We are trusting God's timing and purpose for us, especially when we are in that holding pattern of our lives as we can see in the fall as the leaves begin to change but have not quite fallen to the ground. Or in the spring as bulbs form but do not blossom until it is their time. Those in between seasons where it's not harvest time and it's not sowing time either, but it's waiting time. That season is where patience and trust are working us in the process. They are God's tools in His process of growth for us rather than our tools for manipulating what we want from God.

But you must learn to endure everything, so that you will be completely mature and not lacking in anything (James 1:4 CEVUK00).

There is a season of being still right where you are, a holding point. The leaves stay right where they are on the trees, connected to their life source, getting nutrients from the trees and the sun. They are sustained there until the fall season comes, and they move into the next season of their process. See where I'm going? Don't be in such a rush to move into the next season. Let patience and trust work in you until God says it is time. What we do not want is to get out the flow of the process and step into a season too soon.

We won't be sustained there if we get there too soon. Just like the leaves, we have to stay connected to the life source. We love the shade the leaves provide in the summer and the beauty in the fall. But as spectators, we don't see their process. Others may not see your process, but they get to see your beauty and benefit from you walking in your purpose. It's all worth it to give others hope in their process and to help others through our purpose.

The biggest challenge I found after a major transition like divorce was finding a sense of normal. We can all agree that winter does not feel like fall, and fall does not feel spring. Every season feels different and looks different. But once we make the transition, we change our wardrobe and settle into the temperatures of the new season. I found myself trying to do this with my new life discovery of me. During the separation and after the divorce, the fight for normal was massive! There were so many attempts at just trying to survive that survival mode was mistaken for actual *living*. It was here that coined the phrase: "Learn to live life so it does not live you." Or at least in my mind I coined it. Surviving had become so "normal" that when I began to form a real life and live, it felt so foreign that it felt wrong.

I remember Bishop T. D. Jakes saying that good can feel bad when you are not used to it, and I was not used to it. The best and yet most comedic way I can describe this challenge of getting used to "good" occurred when my godmother took me bra shopping many years ago. I was so used to buying bras wherever. Well she took me for a bra fitting at a department store. When I tried on the first bra the saleswoman picked for me, it was like the skies opened and the angels sang the Hallelujah Chorus! It felt great! So great I wore it out of the store. But in the days after buying it, it felt weird. It took some time getting used to it, but I learned so much from that experience as it comes back to me all these years later.

I learned that new doesn't always mean good. I learned that quality costs and is functional, not ornamental. In other words, like that new bra, my new life had to have quality and functioning support, not just people and things that said they supported me. My new life costs and boy did it ever! It cost me pain, losing people and things, but the support I gained was worth it. Ever since that shopping experience many moons ago, I never went back to cheap, nonfunctioning bras. That is my hope for this next leg of life, no turning back to a life that is cheap and doesn't work.

But the concept of normal was a real challenge. Then I had an epiphany of sorts. In one of our morning chats, God led me to look up the word normal. By definition, normal, an adjective as I was using it, meant "conforming with or constituting a norm or standard or level or type or social norm." Seemed simple enough, but then I read the next definition: "being approximately average or within certain limits in e.g. intelligence and development." Then it hit me. It was like God said, "that is the one I wanted you to see."

To have a normal life meant to have an "approximately average or within certain limits" life. No wonder I was having challenges! And I offer that to you as well. Maybe you are like me, trying to find a sense of normalcy after a whirlwind life of constant change. You can't even build daily or weekly routines without them being interrupted. The only routine I could build in the last five to ten years without interruption was daily conversations with God. Whether it was reading my Bible or in conversation (prayer for most), it was the only consistent thing I could establish without fail. Everything else in my life was subjected to flexibility and interruption. You might be like me, thinking what are you doing wrong? Are you just meant to live a life of constant change?

I offer this to settle your mind and heart because it helped me. You just might be destined for such a life. I don't think God ever wanted us to live an average life with limits, which is what normal means. I don't think He meant for us to be in constant chaos either, but I think there is a striking difference between chaos and things just not being the same. Normalcy offers security. It helps us feel safe in an ever-changing world. When I got married, I thought that was the life I wanted. We lived the typical Christian lifestyle. He worked. I stayed home with the kids. We both were very active in the church. But I had gifts and talents that were not being used. Before long, I found myself starting my own business, which allowed me to serve people in my own capacity, organizing and planning. So what are your gifts and talents that you know you have but are allowing them to lie dormant? Maybe they are the key to your breaking out of the rut of normal.

While safe and secure makes us all feel better, safe and secure aren't really God's way. He is our safety and security, which means that life won't always look certain. Divorce is scary and definitely leads to a great deal of uncertainty and insecurity. It was here that God used a terrible experience to teach me to trust again. I learned to not only trust Him but to trust myself on a whole new level. You can do that, too. Trust yourself again. The closer you get to God, the closer you get to the core of who you are. They work hand in hand.

<u>Reflection</u>

Have you found it hard to accept the new normal of life because you were so used to what always has been? It is time to really see how life has changed for the better even if that better came from something bad happening.

<u>Notes</u>

"To forgive is to set a prisoner free and discover
that the prisoner was you."
-Lewis B. Smedes

11 THE APOLOGY I NEEDED

Earlier in the book, I mentioned a surgery my daughter had
and how it required releasing toxins that developed on her hip.
Without the surgery, she would find herself dealing with other
medical issues, such as arthritis, later in life.

I want to bring that back up because while this journey of
discovery is nowhere near over, there have been some surgeries
along the way that have simply made me better than ever
before. The discovery of being a people pleaser was just the
beginning. I had to accept that was my personality disorder and
then choose to do the work to fix me. I wanted to do the work
more than anything! I was sick of the cycle it played in my life,
and now that I knew what was causing my infection, I wanted
God to do the surgery to remove it. The apostle Paul in his

letters to the church at Philippi mentions his prayers for them, and as he is giving thanks for them, he says, "He who has begun a good work in you will carry it out on to completion until the day of Christ Jesus" (Philippians 1:6). I take this passage and apply it to my own life because this entire journey that I am sharing with you has been about the work that God has been doing in me and His faithfulness to me. There are other meanings to the scripture for all the Bible scholars, but in this moment, this is how I am applying it. God is indeed faithful. God says to Jeremiah (Jeremiah 1:5), "Before I formed you in the womb I knew you, before you were born I set you apart; I appointed you as a prophet to the nations."

If God knew Jeremiah and appointed him, then of course He knew me and appointed me. He knew you and appointed you, too. The surgeries that I have experienced on this journey have removed everything that was not given to me by God, every label, every dysfunction, every experience that was not to be a part of my design and identity. As the healing process began, much like my daughter after her hip surgery, I did not want to step out again. But I knew to test the healing, to put my natural gifts and talents to use for God's intended purpose, I had to gain the courage to step out again and try some new things while returning to some new beginnings.

Beginning anything again is often scary. There is fear of repeating the same mistake you may have made last time. There is fear of not making the best choice. Then there is fear of simply the unknown, which encompasses all of the latter. I remember the moment I realized I had not moved on with my life after the divorce because I was afraid of trying a relationship again. I was content in being on my own, but I knew I wanted another relationship, THE relationship. I knew not just anyone would do, so I found myself being very particular about whom I spent my time with during this season. I would much rather be alone for the right reasons than with someone for the wrong ones. It was here in this place of contentment and valuing myself and my time that I realized I still had a fear of trying something new. Was my fear keeping "him" from finding me? Was I hidden behind that fear so "he" could not get to me? Who else could not get to me because I was hiding? So while I valued my alone time, I knew that was not the only time I would need. As I stated earlier in the book, we need relationships. They teach, nurture, and mature us.

The wonderful thing about God is that He has the perfect timing. He knew when I was ready before I knew. So as any father would, He made sure I had the right people at the right time, and He removed the wrong people at the right time. The relationships that were forming in my life were signs that I was healing properly and most importantly that I was safe in His protection. It changes the game when you KNOW God is protecting you, and it is not just something you are saying because it sounds good.

In this journey of discovery as I found myself getting closer to me, I found that I could be my biggest hindrance. No one could do anything that I did not allow. When I look back over some of my greatest disappointments and my greatest heartbreaks, there were signs and warnings. Sure I could not avoid them all, but some I could. In this new sense of awareness that I had I gained, I did something major that shifted my perspective. I apologized to myself. I looked myself in the mirror and apologized for all the hurt and the pain that I had gone through. Why did I do that? Because waiting on other people to apologize was a wait that forfeited my ability to move forward. Because living as a victim stunted my growth. Because not recognizing the amazing ways that God was protecting me and setting me up for what has started as the best years of my life was prolonging the joy. I took ownership of the past and let people off the hook. I forgave them and forgave myself for the part that I played.

Everybody's level of "sick and tired" is different. What would it take for you to say that you are sick and tired of living in the past, of blaming others for where your life is or is not, of wondering what could be if you could just get over "it"? I am here to tell you that only you can make that choice. When I think about God and His love, I am always careful to give Him His credit at all times. But one day a dear friend reminded me, "Danita, you had to choose." And that is the greatest power you possess. You can choose! You can choose to love or hate. You can choose to live or die. You can choose to forgive or become bitter. There are some things we may not always have a choice in, but another way we can exercise our ability to choose is in our responses to life. You may not have wanted to choose the divorce. You may not have wanted your loved one to choose it. You may not know what time you have on this earth. But you can choose how you will respond to everything.

My ex-husband and I get along beautifully now. It is a true testament of the love of God working in both of our lives. It took some work to get there. It took some tough choices and proper responses, but we did it. He has since remarried, and I adore his wife! She is beautiful, and I can see how they work so well together. I am happy for him, and I pray for them that their marriage grows and stays God-centered. I would not want him to go through the pain of what we went through again. Someday it will be my time again, but I am in no rush. I thank God for protecting me in this time and for preparing me for "him." In the meantime, I enjoy my family and that our children are growing and thriving seeing Mommy and Daddy getting along. I love that we laugh together and look out for each other. We are friends.

I love the place that I'm currently in, and I'm oh so thankful that God saw fit to guide me through the rough terrains of my life and place me in a space where I am closer to Him than I've ever been, and I'm hopeful for my present and my future.

I hope you never fear those mountains in the distance,
Never settle for the path of least resistance,
Livin' might mean takin' chances but they're worth takin',
Lovin' might be a mistake but it's worth makin'.
Don't let some careless heart leave you bitter,
When you come close to sellin' out reconsider,
Give the heavens above more than just a passing glance,
And when you get the choice to sit it out or dance
I hope you dance!

These are the lyrics to one of my all-time favorite songs, "I Hope You Dance" by Lee Ann Womack. It is a great reminder that no matter what happens, don't choose to sit out on life but make sure you stay **IN** life. Live life! Don't let it live you. Share the best of who you are with the people in your world. Dance! Dance! Dance!

<u>Reflection</u>

Taking ownership of the past is a power move. It is exercising your own power to choose how you will respond to the hand life has dealt you so you can be ready for the new hand about to be dealt. Can you do that? Who can you let off the hook by taking your life back from their hands? How can you give yourself the freedom to truly live what this next season of the journey has in store for you?

<u>Notes</u>

ABOUT THE AUTHOR

Danita is a lover of life, love, and all things Jesus. As a mother and divorcee, she has come to discover she has talents in many arenas. Her one passion that can be found in everything she does is helping others.

Writing became her way to get what she was thinking and experiencing out in a healthy way and at the same time help or inspire others. It has been the encouragement of her close circle of friends and family that kept her blogging - but it was a God-inspired vision that gave her the clearance and purpose to write "God, Love, & Divorce".

There is more to come from the journey she has been on.

Connect with Danita at www.dmsanders.com.

www.ingramcontent.com/pod-product-compliance
Lightning Source LLC
LaVergne TN
LVHW021516080426
835509LV00018B/2535